ARMADILLO

by Marjorie Jackson
illustrations by Marilyn Henry

Richard C. Owen Publishers, Inc.
Katonah, New York

An armadillo slept all day
in her leafy bed in a burrow
under a tree.

At sundown she came out of her hole in the ground to search for food.

She dug for juicy roots
with her strong front claws.

She rooted for scorpions, beetles,
and grubs with her snout
and grunted as she worked.

Once, while far from her burrow, the armadillo saw a coyote — what a fright!
She jumped straight up in the air.

Then she raced away.

She quickly burrowed into the soft earth before the coyote could catch her.

When the coyote finally found her,
he tried to pull her out of her hiding place.
But the ridges on her long, scaly tail
locked her in the ground.

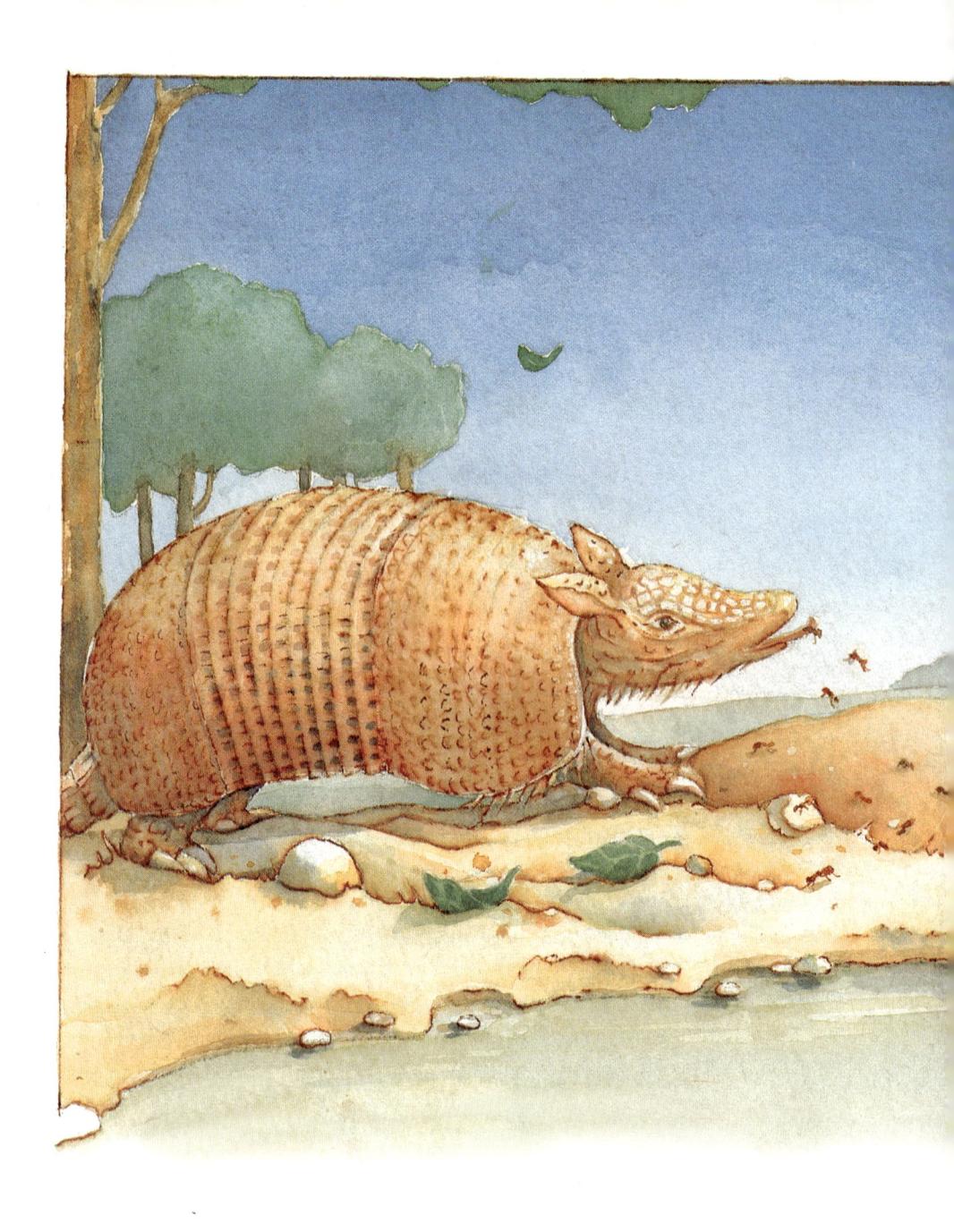

Once, while scooping up fire ants
with her long, sticky tongue,
the armadillo saw a bobcat in the bushes.

She jumped into a nearby creek, closed her nose, held her breath, and waited under the water.

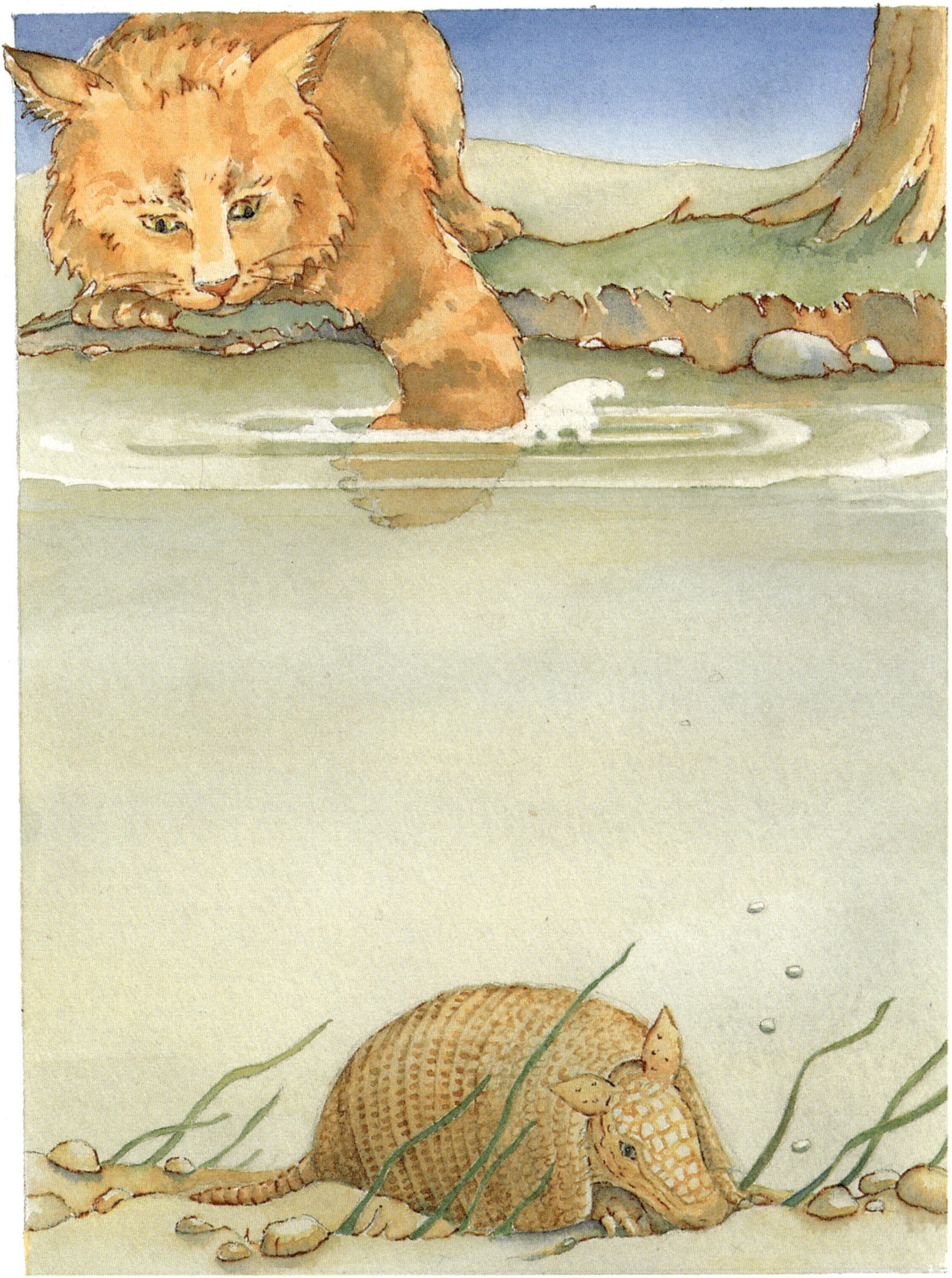

When the danger had passed,
the armadillo strolled back
to her leafy bed under the tree.

Her underground burrow was a safe place.
Here she would one day give birth
to baby armadillos.

Her babies, called *pups,* would all be the same – either four little males or four little females, exactly alike!